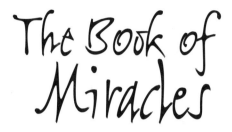

The Book of Miracles

A Young Person's Guide
to Jewish Spiritual Awareness

LAWRENCE KUSHNER

For People of All Faiths, All Backgrounds
JEWISH LIGHTS Publishing
Woodstock, Vermont

The Book of Miracles, 10th Anniversary Edition:
A Young Person's Guide to Jewish Spiritual Awareness

2010 Hardcover Edition, Third Printing

For information regarding permission to reprint material from this book, please mail or fax your request in writing to Jewish Lights Publishing, Permissions Department, at the address / fax number listed below, or e-mail your request to permissions@jewishlights.com.

Library of Congress Cataloging-in-Publication Data
Kushner, Lawrence, 1943–
The book of miracles : a young person's guide to Jewish spiritual awareness / by Lawrence Kushner ; with a new introduction and illustrations by the author. — New 10th anniversary ed.
    p. cm.
Previously published: New York : UAHC Press, c1987.
Summary: A collection of essays which present the elements of Jewish spiritual thinking.
ISBN-13: 978-1-879045-78-1 (hc)
ISBN-10: 1-879045-78-8 (hc)
1. Spiritual life—Judaism—Juvenile literature. 2. Judaism—Essence, genius, nature—Juvenile literature. [1. Judaism. 2. Jewish way of life.] I. Title.
BM723.K867   1997
      296.7'1—dc21   97-35877
                                                CIP
                                                AC

10 9 8 7 6 5 4 3

© 1997 by Lawrence Kushner

Book and jacket design and illustration by Lawrence Kushner
Manufactured in the United States of America

For People of All Faiths, All Backgrounds
Published by Jewish Lights Publishing
A Division of LongHill Partners, Inc.
Sunset Farm Offices, Rte. 4, P.O. Box 237
Woodstock, VT 05091
Tel: (802) 457-4000   Fax: (802) 457-4004
www.jewishlights.com

for David & Elaine
to read to
Jacob, Benjamin and Naomi

Jewish Lights Books by Lawrence Kushner

The Book of Letters: A Mystical Hebrew Alphabet

The Book of Words: Talking Spiritual Life, Living Spiritual Talk

Eyes Remade for Wonder: A Lawrence Kushner Reader

Filling Words with Light:
Hasidic & Mystical Reflections on Jewish Prayer
with Nehemia Polen

God Was in This Place & I, i Did Not Know:
Finding Self, Spirituality and Ultimate Meaning

Honey from the Rock: An Introduction to Jewish Mysticism

Invisible Lines of Connection: Sacred Stories of the Ordinary

Jewish Spirituality: A Brief Introduction for Christians

The River of Light: Jewish Mystical Awareness

The Way Into Jewish Mystical Tradition

For Children

Because Nothing Looks Like God
with Karen Kushner

The Book of Miracles: A Young Person's Guide
to Jewish Spiritual Awareness

How Does God Make Things Happen?
with Karen Kushner
(SkyLight Paths Publishing)

In God's Hands
with Gary Schmidt

What Does God Look Like?
with Karen Kushner
(SkyLight Paths Publishing)

Where Is God?
with Karen Kushner
(SkyLight Paths Publishing)

Fiction

Kabbalah: A Love Story
(Morgan Road Books)

Contents

Introduction to the 10th Anniversary Edition

Some things never go out of vogue. The past decade's fascination with spirituality may have brought it into the spotlight for adults but teaching children about the transcendent has always been a "hot" topic.

What I now find interesting is why adults should bother trying to educate kids about spirituality in the first place. Teaching "spirituality" to children belongs in the same category as teaching them how to play with their food, get fidgety during long speeches or not want to go to sleep at bedtime. Being "spiritual" is something children do naturally. Indeed, we realize with some embarrassment that perhaps it's the children who should be teaching the adults.

No one—of any age—can convincingly answer any of the "big" questions: Is there really a God? What happens when you die? Why do good people suffer? Who made the world? No one knows. Really, no one knows. So what is left to teach? Only increasingly clever ways of asking the questions, posing the problems, surprising the imagination, awakening the soul. And those are things which adults and children can teach one another.

This spirituality business is not about answers, but about ways of *asking* about the meaning of life and creation. A "bad" question slams the door but a "good" question just gets you to wondering and the wondering is wonderful. And as far as I can tell, even with all of their age-appropriate "concrete" thinking, children seem to have as good, if not better, a chance at asking the great unanswerable questions as their parents. Innocence, candor, spontaneity, wonder, amazement, trust, honesty; these are characteristics of children (and the children *within* adults) and they are sources of spiritual thinking for every human being *of any age.*

I suspect now, as I recall the many parents who confessed how they'd go on reading *after their child fell asleep,* that when grownups claim to teach the younger generation, they may be secretly teaching themselves. They fear that somewhere along the line they have lost their own inner child. But since making that admission makes people uncomfortable, they make up this charade of teaching children about spirituality. And this may explain why, over the past decade, adults seem to make up such a large share of the readers of this book, written for 4th through 6th graders!

So, if you're a kid, go easy on the grown-ups; be patient with them; remind them of what it is like to experience life like a youngster. And if you're an adult, wonder again about who made the world.

Foreword

Teaching children about God is like teaching them about sex. We teach them as much of the truth as they can and need to understand and then speak ambiguously about the rest. For centuries, wise parents and teachers, in matters of procreation and piety, have refined equivocation to an art.

These essays attempt to introduce a way of religious thinking that need not be outgrown because it is simplistic or juvenile. Our children, as they begin to think for themselves, may temporarily reject our "parental" piety, but they need not do so because it is unworthy of serious reflection.

Since it lacks many of the classical rubrics of Jewish religious thought, this cannot be systematic theology. Rather, it is an attempt to introduce or reintroduce some elements of Jewish spiritual thinking that lately have been ignored or condemned as heretical.

The perpetual conversation between student and sacred text is the touchstone for the Jewish spiritual tradition. Therefore the primary sources of the stories and insights in this book have been cited. Indeed the measure of success of these short essays will be their ability to entice parent and child, teacher and student, to return to the original texts and enter "the eternal conversation."

In our generation there is much confusion over the meaning of the word "spirituality." The English word "spiritual," which has its roots in Greek and Christian thought, implies a split between the material world and the realm of the spirit. It subtly suggests leaving this everyday, material world in order to enter some other spiritual or holy domain. Classical Hebrew lacks such a distinction; for Jews there is only one world, which is simultaneously material and spiritual. To paraphrase Psalms 24:1, the whole world is full of God. Jewish spirituality is a mode of living in which we are constantly aware of God's presence and purpose.

Part One:

SEEING

CHAPTER 1

Opening Your Eyes

When the people of Israel crossed through the Red Sea, they witnessed a great miracle. Some say it was the greatest miracle that ever happened. On that day they saw a sight more awesome than all the visions of the prophets combined. The sea split and the waters stood like great walls, while Israel escaped to freedom on the distant shore. Awesome. But not for everyone.

Two people, Reuven and Shimon, hurried along among the crowd crossing through the sea. They never once looked up. They noticed only that the ground under their feet was still a little muddy—like a beach at low tide.

"Yucch!" said Reuven, "there's mud all over this place!"

opening your eyes

"Blecch!" said Shimon, "I have muck all over my feet!"

"This is terrible," answered Reuven. "When we were slaves in Egypt, we had to make our bricks out of mud, just like this!"

"Yeah," said Shimon. "There's no difference between being a slave in Egypt and being free here."

And so it went, Reuven and Shimon whining and complaining all the way to freedom. For them there was no miracle. Only mud. Their eyes were closed. They might as well have been asleep. (*Exodus Rabbah* 24:1)

People see only what they understand, not necessarily what lies in front of them. For example, if you saw a television set, you would know what it was and how to operate it. But imagine someone who had never seen a television. To such a person it would be just a strange and useless box. Imagine being in a video store, filled with movies and stories and music, and not even knowing it. How sad when something is right before your eyes, but you are asleep to it. It is like that with our world too.

Something like this once happened to Jacob, our father. He dreamed of a ladder joining heaven and earth. Upon it angels were climbing up and down. Then God appeared and talked to Jacob. When he awoke the next morning, Jacob said to himself, "Wow! God was in this very place all along, and I didn't even know it!" (Genesis 28:16)

Rabbi Shelomo Yitzchaki, who lived in France eight hundred years ago and whom we call Rashi (after the initials of his name), explained what Jacob meant: "If I had known that God would be here, then I wouldn't have gone to sleep!"

To be a Jew means to wake up and to keep your eyes open to the many beautiful, mysterious, and holy things that happen all around us every day. Many of them are like little miracles: when we wake up and see the morning light, when we taste food and grow strong, when we learn from others and grow wise, when we hug the people we love and feel warm, when we help those around us and feel good. All these and more are there for us every day, but we must open our eyes to see them; otherwise we will be like Reuven and Shimon, able to see only mud.

Suppose, right now, your eyes are closed. How do you wake up?

CHAPTER 2

Paying Close Attention

Before Moses was a leader of the Jewish people, he was a shepherd. One day, while tending his flock, he came upon a bush that was burning but didn't burn up. As Moses stared at this awesome sight, God spoke to him for the first time. (Exodus 3:1–6)

People usually explain that God used the burning bush to attract Moses' attention. But suppose you were God and could do anything you wanted—split an ocean, make the sun stand still, or set up a pillar of fire. Compared to such spectacular displays, a burning bush is not very impressive. So why did God choose such a modest miracle?

Maybe the burning bush wasn't a miracle but a test. God wanted to find out if Moses could see mystery in something as ordinary as a little bush on fire. For Moses

Paying Close Attention

had to watch the flames long enough to realize that the branches were not being consumed and that something awesome was happening. Once God saw that Moses could pay attention, God spoke to him.

Much later, when God was ready to give Moses the Torah on Mount Sinai, God said, "Come up to Me on the mountain and be there." (Exodus 24:12) Rabbi Menachem Mendl from the town of Kotzk (whom we call the Kotzker Rebbe) asked: "If God told Moses to come up on the mountain, then why did God also say, 'be there'? Where else would he be?"

The answer, suggests the Kotzker, is that not only did God want Moses to be up on the mountain, God wanted him to pay close attention; otherwise he would not really be there. Often people are physically in a place but, because they are not paying attention, they might as well be somewhere else.

Jews have a special way of remembering to pay attention. It is called a *berachah* or a blessing. It begins, *Baruch atah Adonai,* "Holy One of blessing," *Elohenu melech ha'olam,* "Your presence fills creation." Then we add words appropriate for the occasion like: "who brings forth bread from the earth," or "who removes sleep from my eyes and slumber from my eyelids," or "who spreads the shelter of peace over us."

Each time we say a *berachah*, we say to ourselves, "Pay attention. Something awesome is happening all around us." And then we realize that the ordinary world conceals mysteries.

CHAPTER 3

The One Who Is Hidden Everywhere

If you pay close attention, you will discover that wonders and mysteries are hidden everywhere.

The Baal Shem Tov, the founder of Hasidism, used to tell a story about how God is concealed in the world. Once there was a king who was a master of illusion—he could make people see things that weren't really there. More than anything else, the king wanted his people to come and be close to him. But the people were always too busy. The farmers needed to milk the cows, the sailors had to scrub the decks, and the shopkeepers had to sell their wares. So the lonely king devised a plan.

He built around himself a magnificent but illusory castle. Then he sent out invitations to everyone in his

The One Who is
Hidden Everywhere

kingdom: "You are personally invited to come and be close to the king. But it will not be easy; the king is hidden in a great castle."

"What a challenge," his subjects said, and they hurried to the castle. When they arrived, they found that the walls were high, the windows barred, and the gate bolted. There seemed to be no way to enter. So, one by one, the people gave up and went home. ("It is like that with us, too," the Baal Shem Tov would say. "We start out eagerly looking for God but get distracted easily and give up the search.")

Then one day someone came along and thought, "What if the wall of this castle is only an illusion." She approached the wall, examined it closely, and saw that it was not really there! Nothing stood between herself and the king!

Like the wall, everything in the world—trees, animals, oceans, stars, even people—conceals the One who made it and reveals the One who can be found inside it. King David expressed this when he wrote in one of his psalms, "the whole world and everything in it belong to God." (Psalms 24:1)

Rabbi Menachem Nahum from the Ukrainian town of Chernobyl taught that you can find God's presence everywhere. "There is nothing besides the presence of God...and the presence of the Creator remains in each created thing." If you draw a birthday card for your mother, you are in the card. If you make a gift for your father, you are in that gift. And, if you design and build a house, your presence dwells in that house. We are in what we make. And, because God made the whole universe, God can be found everywhere within it.

When we say that God is everywhere, it does not mean that God is invisible. It means if we look closely, we can find God's presence hidden everywhere because God created everything. And, because God is hidden inside everything, all things are connected to one another.

CHAPTER 4

All Things Are Connected

In the ancient land of Israel there lived a man named Honi. One day Honi saw an old man planting a carob tree and asked, "How long will it take for that tree to bear fruit?"

"Seventy years," replied the man.

"But you are already old; you'll never live that long!" said Honi.

"I know," explained the man, "but my parents and grandparents planted fruit trees for me, so I am planting fruit trees for my children and my grandchildren."

Honi was very impressed by this answer. He sat down behind some nearby rocks to take a short nap. When he awoke, he saw a man gathering carob fruit and asked him how it was possible for newly planted trees to yield fruit in such a short time.

"A short time?" repeated the man in disbelief. "My grandfather planted this tree!"

All Things are connected

"Oh, my God!" thought Honi; "I must have slept for seventy years!" (*Ta'anit* 22b–23a)

Each generation is linked to the next by its actions. We depend on those who came before us, just as someday our children will depend on us. For this reason, all the generations are connected to one another. In the same way generations are linked, we are also connected to all the people around us.

When the children of Israel wandered in the wilderness, they carried a portable temple called the *mishkan*, the wilderness tabernacle. When the work of the *mishkan* was finally completed, the Torah says that "the tabernacle was 'one.'" (Exodus 36:13) Rabbi Mordecai Yosef of the Polish town, Ishbitz, thought that this was an odd thing to say about a building. Perhaps, he suggested, the Torah is not telling us something about the building but about its builders and how they worked.

While building the *mishkan*, all the children of Israel worked as a team. Each person, contributing only one small part, felt as important as every other person. After the *mishkan* was completed, they saw how their individual tasks fit together, as if one person had constructed the whole thing. Realizing how they had depended on one another, they understood that the tabernacle was 'one.' Even the person who made the Holy Ark itself realized that he was no more important than the person who made only the courtyard tent pegs.

We are joined therefore, not only to people who have lived long before us and who will live after we have died, but to people now living, to people we do not know. Invisible lines of depending are everywhere, as if millions of glistening threads tie us to the universe and the universe to us. Nothing is ever detached, alone. We are all parts of one great living organism.

Martin Buber, the great Jewish philosopher who taught in Germany and later in Israel, believed that nothing was more important than the relationship between two people. They can be members of the same family or sometimes even complete strangers. When two individuals realize that they depend on one another, that they are connected to one another, that they have a relationship with one another, then they have come closer to God. Buber imagined that the invisible lines of relation which joined them to one another also joined them to God.

We are all joined to one another, and that "all-joined-togetherness" is an important part of God. When we say the *Shema,* that God is One, we are saying that everything and everyone is connected. And the more we look at our world, the more we realize that it is made according to a master plan, a blueprint.

Part Two:

HEARING

CHAPTER 5

The Blueprint inside Creation

Blueprints are written instructions for constructing a building. They show the design of the completed structure that forever remains within the building. In the same way, sheet music instructs the musician. The notes are on paper but, whenever the melody is played, they are also in the music. If you have ever tried to build a complicated model or play a song on the piano, you understand why it is important to have a plan before you begin.

Scientists have discovered that each person has within every cell of his body a tiny molecule called DNA which contains a genetic code. It is a personal blueprint, a plan for his body—the color of his eyes, the shape of his face, and even how tall he will grow. Our universe also has such a plan.

A Blueprint of Creation

At the beginning of the beginning, God was unable to create the world. No matter how many times and how many different ways God tried to arrange them, the parts wouldn't fit together. The universe kept collapsing because God had no diagram, no design.

God said, "I need an overall plan for My world. I want it to be One, as I am One. I know what I will do," thought God. "I will use Torah as a blueprint for creation and that way all the parts of the world will fit together, and I and My Torah will be inside everything!" (*Pirke de-Rabbi Eliezer* 3)

Long ago our Rabbis understood this. When we read in the Book of Proverbs (8:22) that "God made me as the very first thing," the Rabbis understood "me" to mean that the Torah preceded creation. They did not mean the Sefer Torah we keep in the ark but an idea or a plan which God could use. They discovered this same idea when they realized that there were two ways to translate *b'ray-sheet*, the first Hebrew word in the Book of Genesis.

We usually translate *b'ray-sheet* as "In the beginning." But the Rabbis noticed that the Hebrew letter *bet* doesn't always mean "in"; it can also mean "with." If that is so, then *b'ray-sheet* (as in "In the beginning God created the heavens and the earth") also could be saying, "With *ray-sheet* God created the heavens and the earth." And this would mean, suggested the Rabbis, that *ray-sheet* must be another name for Torah. In other words, God created the world with Torah. Torah is God's blueprint for the world. (*Genesis Rabbah* 1:1)

One rabbinic legend says that the words of Torah are spoken continuously from Mount Sinai without interruption. (*Pirke Avot* 6:2; *Exodus Rabbah* 41:7) We cannot hear the voice because of the noise and distractions all around us. Even when we shut off the television and ask everyone in the room to be silent, even when we stop making sounds ourselves, there is still the distracting "noise" of thinking going on inside our own heads. And that is what made Mount Sinai so special: God hushed the world to perfect silence.

When God gave the Torah, no bird chirped and no fowl flew, the wind and sea stood still, and the angels stopped singing, "Holy, holy, holy." Once there was complete silence, God's voice went forth. (*Exodus Rabbah* 29:9) And everyone could hear the words of Torah that had been there all along.

CHAPTER 6

The Silent Sound of Alef

No one really knows for sure what happened on Mount Sinai. Some people imagine that God dictated the whole Torah, word by word. Others believe that the Ten Commandments were carved in stone with the finger of God. The Torah itself tells different stories. Some think that, in addition to the Torah, God also whispered the Talmud to Moses. Some believe that God did not speak or write; rather, God inspired Moses. And there are even those who think that Moses imagined the whole thing.

At different times you may have believed one or another explanation. That is the Jewish way. Something as important as how God talks to people and what God says is certain to get Jews arguing. But, no matter what our interpretation, we all agree that what happened on Mount Sinai was a very important Jewish event.

The Soundless Aleph

Once several Jews were having just such an argument. The first one claimed that God gave the whole Torah, word by word. A second one said that God gave only the ten sayings, commonly called the Ten Commandments.

A third person remembered the old legend from the Talmud (*Makot* 23a–b) which tells that God didn't give ten but only the first two sayings ("I am the Lord your God…" and "You shall not have any other gods beside Me…"). "After all," that person suggested, "the first two sayings are the basis for all of Judaism. One who remembers that there is a God who frees people and that there are no other gods will probably be religious." A fourth person said that God uttered only the first saying, "I am the Lord your God." The four agreed that, if God had given only one saying, it would have been the most important one—that there is a God.

"No. God didn't even say that much!" insisted a fifth person. "All God said was the first word of the first saying, 'I' [in Hebrew, *Anochi*]." All five then agreed that, if God had said only one word, it would have been *Anochi* because it affirms the importance of the self.

Then Rabbi Mendl Torum of Rymanov, who had been listening to all of this, came forward and said, "Not even the first word. All God said was the first letter of the first word of the first saying—which in Hebrew is also the first letter of the alphabet, *Alef*."

"But we thought that the *Alef* was a silent letter," replied the others.

"Almost, but not perfectly silent," answered Rabbi Mendl. "You see, *Alef* makes a tiny, little sound that is the beginning of every sound. Open your mouth and begin to make a sound. Stop! That is *Alef*. God made the voice of *Alef* so quiet that if you made any other noise you wouldn't be able to hear it. At Sinai all the people of Israel needed to hear was the sound of *Alef*. It meant that God and the Jewish people could have a conversation."

The Zohar, the most important set of Jewish mystical books, teaches that *Alef*—the almost sound of the first letter of the first word of the first saying—contains the whole Torah. (Zohar II:85b) But not everyone hears the gentle sound of *Alef*. People are able to hear only what they are ready to hear. God speaks to each of us in a personal way, taking into consideration our strength, wisdom, and preparation. In one midrash on the Book of Exodus, both Moses and his brother Aaron heard the same word from God. To Moses, it said, "Go to Egypt to free the Jews." To Aaron, who was already in Egypt, it said, "Go into the wilderness to meet your brother Moses; he needs your help."

The Midrash describes God's voice as so powerful and frightening that God tempers it by creating different sounds for each person. There was even a special sounding voice just for the ears of small children. (*Exodus Rabbah* 5:9)

CHAPTER 7

The Never-ending Understanding

Because we each hear the words of Torah in a unique way, we Jews often argue about their meaning. Often when we argue, it means we are fighting, but, when Jews disagree or argue about the meaning of Torah, we are actually helping one another to become better Jews.

What does it mean, for example, when the Torah says that "God created the world in six days"? Could it mean that, before there was a sun or an earth, there were twenty-four-hour days just as we have now? Or is it teaching that every week our world is created anew and that on Shabbat we should stop creating, just as God stopped?

In Hebrew such an argument is called *l'shaym shamayim,* an argument for the sake of heaven or an

Never Ending Understanding

argument for God's sake. (*Pirke Avot* 5:17) Trying to understand the Torah is an endless search; no matter how many times we reread it, or how many times we are sure we understand it, a new interpretation will arise to challenge our understanding.

Not even Moses himself understood everything in the Torah. According to the Talmud, when Moses went up on Mount Sinai, he found God adding some finishing touches to the Torah. God was drawing *tagin*, little decorative crowns, on some of the letters.

"What are you doing?" asked Moses. "I thought the Torah was already complete. How come you're adding those little crowns on some of the letters?"

"Centuries from now there will be students and teachers," answered God, "who will see in each little crown all kinds of wonderful laws and enchanting stories."

"May I visit those students and teachers?" asked Moses.

"Just turn around," replied God.

Moses found himself in a classroom where students were studying Torah. Invisible, Moses walked to the back row and sat down, but he was unable to understand what they were learning. After a few minutes, one of the students asked the teacher about the meaning of a certain passage. The teacher replied, "I am not sure what these words mean, but we will study them anyway because we must try to remember everything Moses taught us."

At first Moses felt honored and proud. Then, with a troubled look on his face, he turned to God and said, "The students and teachers in this class are so wise, and yet You chose me to deliver Your Torah!"

God replied, "Not even you, Moses, can understand everything in the Torah." (*Menachot* 29b)

Every generation finds new meaning in the Torah. In trying to understand its teachings, we make ourselves better Jews. Our people have never found a better way of learning about God and of coming close to God. Everything we learn and everything we are as Jews comes from Torah. Nearly two thousand years ago, a wise teacher named Ben Bag Bag said, "Study the Torah and study it again and again, because everything you need to know is in it." (*Pirke Avot* 5:22)

CHAPTER 8

An Orchard of Delicious Words

How could everything you need to know be contained in the Torah, in only five books? Long ago our teachers realized that the Torah is like a beautiful orchard. From a distance you see only a field of trees. When you come closer, you see that each has leaves, blossoms, and fruit. When you come even closer, you realize that each fruit is covered by a skin. And, if you are persistent and peel back the skin, your reward is a delicious treat. Now you realize that what at first seemed to be only a field of trees actually conceals layers within layers of wonderful things.

The Hebrew word for orchard is *pardes*, spelled: *pey, resh, dalet, samech.* Each one of these letters stands for a layer of the Torah. The letter *pey* is the first letter of *peshat,* which means the simple story, the one you find if you

An Orchard of Words

just read the Torah quickly without much thought. When Adam disobeyed God and ate from the tree of knowledge, he was ashamed, so he hid himself. (Genesis 3:8–10) That is the simple story.

The letter *resh* is the first letter of *remez*, which means hint. If you think about a story or a word in the Torah, it usually will lead to your thinking about something else. As you wonder what the word means, you might notice that it reminds you of something you have thought about or done in the past. Perhaps, like Adam, you once did something you were ashamed of and tried to hide. Adam's story hints at something in your life.

The letter *dalet* is the first letter of *derash*, which means interpreting. Some of the lessons in the story may remind you of other stories in the Torah which, in turn, can teach you about your life. If God knows where Adam is hiding, then why ask him, "Where are you?" Perhaps God wants Adam to realize that, when he tries to hide from God, he is hiding only from himself.

The letter *samech* is the first letter of *sod*, which means secret. This layer is "secret," not because it cannot be told, but because, even when seen, its meaning remains mysterious. Only an advanced student of Torah can understand the "secret" meaning when God says, "Yesterday, Adam, you were so big that you extended from one end of the universe to the other, but now, after you have sinned, you can hide among the trees of the garden." (*Genesis Rabbah* 19:9)

Taken all together, *pey, resh, dalet,* and *samech* (the simple, the hint, the interpreting, and the secret) spell PaRDeS, orchard. The Torah, the source book of Judaism, is like an orchard; it conceals many wonderful and delicious surprises. But, more than that, it tells us everything we, as Jews, need to know and do. By telling us how to live, the Torah gives us life. Just as we read in the Book of Proverbs (3:18), "It is a tree of life to those who hold on to it."

Part Three:

DOING

CHAPTER 9

Doing and Understanding

Seeing the wonders of creation everywhere is one way to know about God. Studying the words of Torah is another. But sometimes we are unable to see miracles, and the words of Torah may be too difficult to understand. Fortunately, there is a third way for a Jew to know about God: doing what we believe God wants us to do. But how do we know what God wants?

A curious phrase in the Book of Exodus (24:7) offers a clue. When God offers the Torah to the children of Israel, we do not say, "Let us hear what God wants and then we'll do it." Instead, we say, "We will do and we will hear." A well-known midrash offers a fascinating explaination for this strange answer.

God offered the commandments, in turn, to each of the peoples of the earth. First God went to the children of Edom and said, "Would you like My commandments?"

"It's for you."

They said, "That depends on what they say."

"One says, 'You cannot steal things,'" replied God.

"Are You kidding!" the Edomites replied. "We steal all the time. It's one of the best things about being a Edomite! Give Your commandments to someone else."

When God tried the Moabites, they too insisted on first knowing what the commandments say. So God told them, "You have to honor your parents."

"No way," said the Moabites. "We love to give our parents a hard time. You can keep Your commandments."

God was getting discouraged. One by one, the peoples demanded to know the commandments in advance, and, one by one, they refused.

Ready to give up, God decided to try one last group, the children of Israel. "Would you like to have My commandments?"

"Your commandments! Fantastic! We'll do whatever they say, even before we know what they are. Let us have them. We'll do and we'll hear." (*Pesikta Rabbati* 21)

When Rabbi Menachem Mendl of Kotzk read in Exodus, "We will do and we will hear," he explained that some actions cannot be understood (heard) until they are performed (done). By doing we understand. If the Edomites had tried not stealing or the Moabites had tried honoring their parents, they might have understood what a great treasure God was offering them.

Making Shabbat, giving to the poor, and all the other commandments, mitzvot, in the Torah are not simply impersonal, ancient religious laws. The mitzvot, explained Franz Rosenzweig, a great German Jewish teacher, are addressed to each one of us personally. We do mitzvot because we believe God calls on us to do them.

My teacher, Rabbi Arnold Jacob Wolf, described the following scene: Jews are walking along a street studded with precious stones. They pull the gems from the pavement and put them into their knapsacks. Some are easily plucked from the pavement; others remain stuck. It is like that with the mitzvot—some, like honoring parents or helping others, are easy; others, like attending services every Shabbat or not gossiping, are more difficult.

When we perform a mitzvah, we make it ours. We understand it; we "hear" it. It becomes part of us. Performing a mitzvah changes us, brings us closer to God. It also has the mysterious power to repair what is broken.

CHAPTER 10

Repairing the World

In the sixteenth-century town of Tsefat, Rabbi Isaac Luria observed that in his world, like ours, many things seemed to be wrong. People suffered from hunger, disease, hatred, and war. "How could God allow such terrible things to happen?" wondered Luria. "Perhaps," he suggested, "it is because God needs our help." He explained his answer with a mystical story.

When first setting out to make the world, God planned to pour a Holy Light into everything in order to make it real. God prepared vessels to contain the Holy Light. But something went wrong. The light was so bright that the vessels burst, shattering into millions of broken pieces like dishes dropped on the floor. The Hebrew phrase which Luria used for this "breaking of the vessels" is *sh'virat ha-kaylim*.

Repairing the World

Our world is a mess because it is filled with broken fragments. When people fight and hurt one another, they allow the world to remain shattered. The same can be said of people who have pantries filled with food and let others starve. According to Luria, we live in a cosmic heap of broken pieces, and God cannot repair it alone.

That is why God created us and gave us freedom of choice. We are free to do whatever we please with our world. We can allow things to remain broken or, as Luria urged, we can try to repair the mess. Luria's Hebrew phrase for "repairing the world" is *tikun olam.*

As Jews, our most important task in life is to find what is broken in our world and repair it. The commandments in the Torah instruct us, not only on how to live as Jews, but on how to mend creation.

At the very beginning of the Book of Genesis (2:15) we read that God put Adam and Eve in the Garden of Eden and told them not to eat from the tree of knowledge. God also told them that it was their job to take care of the garden and to protect it.

The stories in the Torah tell not only of what happened long ago but also of what happens in each generation. The stories happen over and over again in the life of each person. The Garden of Eden is our world, and we are Adam and Eve. When God says, "Take care of the garden and protect it," God says to us, "Take care of your world and protect it."

According to one midrash, God showed Adam and Eve the Garden of Eden and said, "I have made the whole thing for you, so please take good care of it. If you wreck it, there will be no one else to repair it other than you." (*Ecclesiastes Rabbah* 7:13)

When you see something that is broken, fix it. When you find something that is lost, return it. When you see something that needs to be done, do it. In that way, you will take care of your world and repair creation. If all the people in the world were to do so, our world would truly be a Garden of Eden, the way God meant it to be. If everything broken could be repaired, then everyone and everything would fit together like the pieces of one gigantic jigsaw puzzle. But, for people to begin the great task of repairing creation, they first must take responsibility for what they do.

CHAPTER 11

Taking Responsibility

Taking responsibility means saying, "I can see that something is wrong. If it is my fault, I admit it and I am sorry. If it is not my fault, I will do what I can to help make things better."

After Adam and Eve disobeyed God and ate from the fruit of the tree, they were ashamed. Because they were afraid to take responsibility for what they had done, they hid themselves. Hiding is the opposite of taking responsibility.

There are many ways of hiding. We can pretend that we don't see what is wrong: a mess to be cleaned up or the sadness of someone who needs extra loving. We say to ourselves, "I am too busy" or "I am too tired to help." It is as if we simply close our eyes and ears to what needs to be done. When we act like this, we are hiding from our responsibility.

Taking Responsibility

Other times, we see what is wrong around us but we say, "This has nothing to do with me; it is not my problem." This is just another way of hiding from our responsibility.

Still another way is to blame someone else. When God came to Adam and Eve and asked them what had happened, Adam blamed Eve. Eve blamed the snake. They each said, "It's not my fault!" We, too, sometimes blame our brothers and sisters, our parents, our enemies, and our friends. We even try to blame God.

But God says, "It's your world. You are free to do with it as you choose. I cannot make you do what I want. If I did, then you would be nothing more than a puppet. Instead, I will tell you what is right and wrong. You are then free to choose for yourself how to act. If you make the world a beautiful garden, it will be a tribute to you. But, if you spoil the world-garden, it will be your shame. Just remember that I will hold you responsible for what you do."

If people choose to spend their money and time making terrible weapons instead of curing terrible diseases, it is their choice, not the will of God. They, like Adam and Eve, are only hiding from their responsibility to repair the world.

In Genesis (3:9), God asks Adam and Eve what seems to be a strange question, "Where are you?" Why would God, who obviously knows where Adam and Eve are hiding, ask them where they were?

The great Italian Bible teacher, Umberto Cassuto, compares this passage to a father's coming to scold his child who has misbehaved. Seeing the disappointment on the father's face, the child hides behind the door. The father knows where his child is hiding but, nevertheless, calls out to his child, "Where are you?" He is really saying, "Please, come out and face me!"

When something goes wrong, a little child often pretends not to notice, blames someone else, or hides. Older children learn to take more responsibility when things go wrong. Ideally, adults try to take responsibility at all times, even when they would like to hide. A responsible adult says, "God has given me these hands to do what needs to be done."

CHAPTER 12

The Hands of God

The following story is told by my teacher, Rabbi Zalman Schachter Shalomi.

A long time ago in the northern part of Israel, in the town of Tsefat, the richest man in town was sleeping, as usual, through Shabbat morning services. Every now and then, he would almost wake up, trying to get comfortable on the hard wooden bench, and then sink back into a deep sleep. One morning he awoke just long enough to hear the chanting of the Torah verses from Leviticus 24:5–6 in which God instructs the children of Israel to place twelve loaves of chalah on a table in the ancient wilderness tabernacle.

When services ended, the wealthy man woke up, not realizing that all he had heard was the Torah reading about how God wanted twelve loaves of chalah. He thought that God had come to him in his sleep and had asked him

The Hands of God

personally to bring twelve loaves of chalah to God. The rich man felt honored that God should single him out, but he also felt a little foolish. Of all the things God could want from a person, twelve loaves of chalah did not seem very important. But who was he to argue with God. He went home and baked the bread.

Upon returning to the synagogue, he decided the only proper place for his holy gift was alongside the Torah scrolls in the ark. He carefully arranged the loaves and said to God, "Thank You for telling me what You want of me. Pleasing You makes me very happy." Then he left.

No sooner had he gone than the poorest Jew in the town, the synagogue janitor, entered the sanctuary. All alone, he spoke to God. "O Lord, I am so poor. My family is starving; we have nothing to eat. Unless You perform a miracle for us, we will surely perish." Then, as was his custom, he walked around the room to tidy it up. When he ascended the bimah and opened the ark, there before him were twelve loaves of chalah! "A miracle!" exclaimed the poor man, "I had no idea You worked so quickly! Blessed are You, O God, who answers our prayers." Then he ran home to share the bread with his family.

Minutes later, the rich man returned to the sanctuary, curious to know whether or not God ate the chalah.

Slowly he ascended the bimah, opened the ark, and saw that the chalot were gone. "Oh, my God!" he shouted, "You really ate my chalot! I thought You were teasing. This is wonderful. You can be sure that I'll bring another twelve loaves—with raisins in them too!"

The following week, the rich man brought a dozen loaves to the synagogue and again left them in the ark. Minutes later, the poor man entered the sanctuary. "God, I don't know how to say this, but I'm out of food again. Seven loaves we ate, four we sold, and one we gave to charity. But now, nothing is left and, unless You do another miracle, we surely will starve." He approached the ark and slowly opened its doors. "Another miracle!" he cried, "twelve more loaves, and with raisins too! Thank You God; this is wonderful!"

The chalah exchange became a weekly ritual that continued for many years. And, like most rituals that become routine, neither man gave it much thought. Then, one day, the rabbi, detained in the sanctuary longer than usual, watched the rich man place the dozen loaves in the ark and the poor man redeem them.

The rabbi called the two men together and told them what they had been doing.

"I see," said the rich man sadly, "God doesn't really eat chalah."

"I understand," said the poor man, "God hasn't been baking chalah for me after all."

They both feared that now God no longer would be present in their lives.

Then the rabbi asked them to look at their hands. "Your hands," he said to the rich man, "are the hands of God giving food to the poor. And your hands," said the rabbi to the poor man, "also are the hands of God, receiving gifts from the rich. So you see, God can still be present in your lives. Continue baking and continue taking. Your hands are the hands of God."

Part Four:

PERSON

CHAPTER 13

The Self of the Universe

Talking about God can lead to confusion and contradiction: God is like a person but has no body. God is everywhere but dwells in heaven.

One reason we find talking about God so difficult is that we are part of what we are trying to understand. We cannot separate ourselves completely from God, and, therefore, we can never comprehend the totality. It would be like trying to look at our own eyes without a mirror.

In the first tractate of the Talmud, Rabbi Shimi considers what King David meant in the Book of Psalms (103:1) when he said, "Bless the Lord, O my soul."

King David must have been referring to his innermost self. Just as God fills the whole world, so the self fills the body. Just as God sees but is not seen, so the self sees but is not seen. Just as God nourishes the whole world, so

The Self of the Universe

the self nourishes the whole body. Just as God dwells in the innermost part of everything, so the self dwells in the innermost part of each person. (*Berachot* 10a) This does not mean that God is the universe or that we are God. Rather, God is the Self of the universe.

Professor Richard Rubenstein once tried to explain God by saying that God is like the ocean and we are like the waves. The waves seem to be separate from the ocean, rising and falling on their own. But, though they seem to be separate, the waves are made of the ocean and never exist apart from it. Of course the ocean is more than the total of all the waves, but we can still learn a lot about it from watching the waves. In the same way, we learn most of what we know about God from people.

Another way of thinking about God is to imagine that God is like a river made of light, flowing softly within all creation. In the Book of Psalms (36:10), King David says, "God, You are the fountain of life; by Your light do we see light." Since we are made of this light, we cannot see it. But it flows within us, joining us with everything in the universe.

The most important thing we can say about God is that "God is One." As it says in Deuteronomy 6:4, "Hear,

O Israel: the Lord is our God, the Lord is One!" When we say the *Shema*, we remind ourselves that all of creation, in all its parts—mountains, ants, clouds, friends, songs, hugs, teeth, everything—share some One in common. The Holy One of Being. The Only One of Being.

CHAPTER 14

The Whirlwind

If God dwells within all creation, then God is what life is made of. For this reason, when we are keenly aware of being alive, we also feel God's presence. We sense a special closeness to God when someone is born, just as we do when someone dies. This does not necessarily mean that God causes people to be born or to die.

The ways of God are beyond human understanding. Only the experience of living can begin to give some insight. Simple formulas such as good people will be rewarded and bad people will be punished often do not hold true in real life.

The Book of Job teaches us about suffering and the mystery of knowing God. Job is the story of a righteous man whose happy life suddenly turns miserable. His business fails, his children die, and he is afflicted with terrible diseases.

The Whirlwind

Despite his ordeal, Job never curses God. His friends believed that bad things happen only as God's punishment for sin, that Job suffers because he must have done something wrong. They try to convince him to apologize to God, but Job refuses, knowing he has acted justly. Heartbroken and angry, he sits alone on a pile of ashes, wishing he had never been born.

Finally, at the very end of the book, from out of a whirlwind, God asks Job one question after another: "Where were you when I laid the foundations of the universe? Have you commanded the morning to begin? Have you entered the bottom of the ocean? Do you know the way to the home of light? If you know, tell Me." (Job 38:4, 12, 16, 17, 18) Job realizes that he knows very little about the mysteries of creation and that it is awesome simply to be alive. Suddenly he feels grateful just to be able to love, to learn, and to live. Once that happens, the blessings and happiness of his life are restored.

When you were a child, your parents punished you when you were bad and rewarded you when you were good. Now that you are older, you have learned that doing good is its own reward. It feels good to do good.

It is the same way with God as we grow older. We realize that, while God cares very much about how we act, God neither punishes people who are bad nor rewards people who are good. Instead, God seems to say, "Try to make your world the way I have taught you and that will bring you more happiness than the greatest reward you could ever imagine."

CHAPTER 15

Praying God's Prayers

Rabbi Dov Baer, the great storyteller (or *Magid*) of the Polish town, Mezritch, used to say that a person is like a shofar! A shofar sounds only when breath is blown through it; we can only say prayers because God moves through us.

Like God, the prayers are everywhere, but they need mouths and hands to give them melody and movement. Without us, they would flow unnoticed through the universe. People are the instruments that transform prayers into music and words.

The Book of Psalms is one of our biggest and oldest collections of prayer-poems. Its words, like the words of other prayers in our prayer book, are a script or a musical score for words and songs which already exist within each of us and within all creation. One psalm verse (104:24), for example, reads, "How awesome is what You do, God;

Praying God's Prayers—

You have made everything with wisdom; the earth is full of Your creations." These words, recited for generations, are already in the universe, whether or not we say them. If we say them, however, we understand a little more about the mystery of being alive.

Sometimes the prayers seem to come from our own heart; other times we find them written in the prayer book; still other times they seem to be whispered by the wind. But, no matter where we find them, the words of prayers are already present. They need someone to speak them. By giving them a voice, we come closer to God.

Rabbi Kalonymos Kalmish Shapiro of Piesetzna, who died in the Warsaw ghetto, taught that "not only does God hear our prayers but God also says our prayers through us as well." God's words become ours.

Praying connects us to God, and, since God is also connected to everything else, prayer joins us to all creation. Abraham Joshua Heschel, one of the great spiritual teachers of our generation, explained that, in prayer, we realize that our "self is not the hub, but the spoke of the revolving wheel." Such a feeling is so important that Jews devote an entire day of every week to it.

CHAPTER 16

Being Where You Are

A Sefer Torah is written without vowels. We have to fill them in mentally as we read. Someone who understands Hebrew and has a rough idea of the story can usually figure out the vowels. But occasionally a word appears that can be read in different ways, depending on the vowels we add.

Such a word occurs in Genesis 2:1. The letters *vav, yod, chaf, lamed, vav* are usually given vowels so that they are pronounced *vaye'chu-lu*, which means "were finished." Taken in this manner, the verse reads: "The heaven and the earth *were finished...*"

In the Talmud, however, Rabbi Hamnuna notices that, by adding different vowels, the letters *vav, yod, chaf, lamed, vav* could also be pronounced *vaye'cha-lu*, which means "and they finished." Taken in this manner, the verse

Being where you are

reads: "*And they finished* the heaven and the earth." (*Shabbat* 119b)

This raises another question: Who were the "they" who finished the heaven and the earth? Rabbi Hamnuna says that the "they" refers to God and people. Not only do we help God by caring for and repairing creation, we also join God on the eve of every Shabbat by finishing our work.

Why is it so important to be finished? Perhaps because every unfinished task—yesterday's homework, household chores, someone we need to forgive, a hobby project—demands a piece of our attention. It wants us to be "back in yesterday," worrying about what we didn't finish, or it wants us to be "already in tomorrow," worrying about what we still need to do. And whenever we are "back in yesterday" or "already in tomorrow," we are not fully here. Our bodies are obviously present, but our attention is somewhere else.

To make Shabbat, we must, therefore, either finish our work, as God did, or say to ourselves, "Even if it's not done, I'm going to pretend it's done anyway." On Shabbat, I do not worry about what I didn't finish yesterday or what I must do tomorrow; I'm going to be right here.

Each week, on Shabbat I will enjoy some special time, remaining where I am, opening my eyes to the wonder and miracle of creation.

Rabbi Isaac lived in the city of Cracow. He was very poor so, when he dreamed three times in a row about a great treasure buried under a bridge in the distant city of Prague, he set out on the journey to find it. When he arrived in Prague, he discovered that the place he had seen in the dream was patrolled day and night by the king's guards. He circled the spot, watching it from a distance until one day the guards noticed him. When the captain called to Rabbi Isaac and demanded to know what he was doing there, the rabbi told him about the dream.

"You mean to tell me that you believe in such dreams!" laughed the captain. "If I believed in them, I would have to go all the way to Cracow and find some rabbi named Isaac, because I have dreamed that a great treasure lies buried beneath his bed!" Rabbi Isaac thanked the captain, returned home, pushed aside his bed, and dug up the treasure that had been there all along.

What we are seeking is not in the past or in the future. It is not far away or in the possession of someone else. It is exactly where we are and every seventh day, on Shabbat, the miracles of creation can be ours.

Afterword

The goal of spirituality is the bringing together of seeing, hearing, and doing into one whole person. It is to see yourself mirrored in the heavens above and to realize that the Holy One created you personally to help complete the work of repairing the world.

Being "mirrored in the heavens" means that, since the heavens are always overhead, you have an intimate relationship with God—even closer than you can imagine. Being "created to repair the world" means that, since so much in the world is still broken, God is also far away— even farther than you thought. Being "mirrored in the heavens" reminds us of God's presence; being "created to repair the world" reminds us of God's purpose.

To be aware of God's presence and God's purpose sounds like a beautiful idea, but who could remember it even most of the time. There are so many distractions and other matters competing for our attention. At the time each one of them seems important. For this reason, ever since Abraham and Sarah, our people have invented ways to try to remain spiritually aware, every day.

Our people created a tradition filled with songs, stories, legends, and laws to help them remember. That ancient, mysterious, and holy tradition, designed to help us remember about God's presence in our lives and God's purpose for our world, is called Judaism.

Lawrence Kushner
Erev Shabbat
Vayakhel-Pekude 5747
Sudbury, Massachusetts

Bar/Bat Mitzvah

The JGirl's Guide: The Young Jewish Woman's Handbook for Coming of Age
By Penina Adelman, Ali Feldman, and Shulamit Reinharz This inspirational, interactive guidebook helps pre-teen Jewish girls address the many issues surrounding coming of age. 6 x 9, 240 pp, Quality PB, 978-1-58023-215-9 **$14.99** *For ages 11 & up*
  Also Available: **The JGirl's Teacher's and Parent's Guide**
  8½ x 11, 56 pp, PB, 978-1-58023-225-8 **$8.99**

Bar/Bat Mitzvah Basics, 2nd Edition: A Practical Family Guide to Coming of Age
  Together *Edited by Cantor Helen Leneman* 6 x 9, 240 pp, Quality PB, 978-1-58023-151-0 **$18.95**
The Bar/Bat Mitzvah Memory Book, 2nd Edition: An Album for Treasuring the
  Spiritual Celebration *By Rabbi Jeffrey K. Salkin and Nina Salkin*
  8 x 10, 48 pp, 2-color text, Deluxe HC, ribbon marker, 978-1-58023-263-0 **$19.99**
For Kids—Putting God on Your Guest List, 2nd Edition: How to Claim the
  Spiritual Meaning of Your Bar or Bat Mitzvah *By Rabbi Jeffrey K. Salkin*
  6 x 9, 144 pp, Quality PB, 978-1-58023-308-8 **$15.99** *For ages 11–13*

Putting God on the Guest List, 3rd Edition: How to Reclaim the Spiritual
  Meaning of Your Child's Bar or Bat Mitzvah *By Rabbi Jeffrey K. Salkin*
  6 x 9, 224 pp, Quality PB, 978-1-58023-222-7 **$16.99**; HC, 978-1-58023-260-9 **$24.99**
  Also Available: **Putting God on the Guest List Teacher's Guide**
  8½ x 11, 48 pp, PB, 978-1-58023-226-5 **$8.99**
Tough Questions Jews Ask: A Young Adult's Guide to Building a Jewish Life
  By Rabbi Edward Feinstein 6 x 9, 160 pp, Quality PB, 978-1-58023-139-8 **$14.99** *For ages 11 & up*
  Also Available: **Tough Questions Jews Ask Teacher's Guide**
  8½ x 11, 72 pp, PB, 978-1-58023-187-9 **$8.95**

Spirituality/Lawrence Kushner

The Book of Letters: A Mystical Hebrew Alphabet
  Popular HC Edition, 6 x 9, 80 pp, 2-color text, 978-1-879045-00-2 **$24.95**
  Collector's Limited Edition, 9 x 12, 80 pp, gold-foil-embossed pages, w/ limited-edition silkscreened print, 978-1-879045-04-0 **$349.00**

The Book of Miracles: A Young Person's Guide to Jewish Spiritual Awareness
  6 x 9, 96 pp, 2-color illus., HC, 978-1-879045-78-1 **$16.95** *For ages 9–13*

The Book of Words: Talking Spiritual Life, Living Spiritual Talk
  6 x 9, 160 pp, Quality PB, 978-1-58023-020-9 **$16.95**

Eyes Remade for Wonder: A Lawrence Kushner Reader *Introduction by Thomas Moore*
  6 x 9, 240 pp, Quality PB, 978-1-58023-042-1 **$18.95**

Filling Words with Light: Hasidic and Mystical Reflections on Jewish Prayer
  By Rabbi Lawrence Kushner and Rabbi Nehemia Polen
  5½ x 8½, 176 pp, Quality PB, 978-1-58023-238-8 **$16.99**; HC, 978-1-58023-216-6 **$21.99**

God Was in This Place & I, i Did Not Know: Finding Self, Spirituality and
  Ultimate Meaning 6 x 9, 192 pp, Quality PB, 978-1-879045-33-0 **$16.95**

Honey from the Rock: An Introduction to Jewish Mysticism
  6 x 9, 176 pp, Quality PB, 978-1-58023-073-5 **$16.95**

Invisible Lines of Connection: Sacred Stories of the Ordinary
  5½ x 8¼, 160 pp, Quality PB, 978-1-879045-98-9 **$15.95**

Jewish Spirituality: A Brief Introduction for Christians
  5½ x 8¼, 112 pp, Quality PB, 978-1-58023-150-3 **$12.95**

The River of Light: Jewish Mystical Awareness
  6 x 9, 192 pp, Quality PB, 978-1-58023-096-4 **$16.95**

The Way Into Jewish Mystical Tradition
  6 x 9, 224 pp, Quality PB, 978-1-58023-200-5 **$18.99**; HC, 978-1-58023-029-2 **$21.95**

Or phone, fax, mail or e-mail to: **JEWISH LIGHTS Publishing**
Sunset Farm Offices, Route 4 • P.O. Box 237 • Woodstock, Vermont 05091
Tel: (802) 457-4000 • Fax: (802) 457-4004 • www.jewishlights.com
Credit card orders: (800) 962-4544 (8:30AM–5:30PM ET Monday–Friday)
Generous discounts on quantity orders. SATISFACTION GUARANTEED. Prices subject to change.

Children's Books by Sandy Eisenberg Sasso

Adam & Eve's First Sunset: God's New Day

Engaging new story explores fear and hope, faith and gratitude in ways that will delight kids and adults—inspiring us to bless each of God's days and nights.

9 x 12, 32 pp, Full-color illus., HC, 978-1-58023-177-0 **$17.95** *For ages 4 & up*

Also Available as a Board Book: **Adam and Eve's New Day**

5 x 5, 24 pp, Full-color illus., Board Book, 978-1-59473-205-8 **$7.99** *For ages 0–4*
(A book from SkyLight Paths, Jewish Lights' sister imprint)

But God Remembered: Stories of Women from Creation to the Promised Land

Four different stories of women—Lilith, Serach, Bityah and the Daughters of Z—teach us important values through their faith and actions.

9 x 12, 32 pp, Full-color illus., Quality PB, 978-1-58023-372-9 **$8.99** *For ages 8 & up*

Cain & Abel: Finding the Fruits of Peace

Shows children that we have the power to deal with anger in positive ways. Provides questions for kids and adults to explore together.

9 x 12, 32 pp, Full-color illus., HC, 978-1-58023-123-7 **$16.95** *For ages 5 & up*

God in Between

If you wanted to find God, where would you look? This magical, mythical tale teaches that God can be found where we are: within all of us and the relationships between us. 9 x 12, 32 pp, Full-color illus., HC, 978-1-879045-86-6 **$16.95** *For ages 4 & up*

God's Paintbrush: Special 10th Anniversary Edition

Wonderfully interactive, invites children of all faiths and backgrounds to encounter God through moments in their own lives. Provides questions adult and child can explore together. 11 x 8½, 32 pp, Full-color illus., HC, 978-1-58023-195-4 **$17.95** *For ages 4 & up*

Also Available as a Board Book: **I Am God's Paintbrush**

5 x 5, 24 pp, Full-color illus., Board Book, 978-1-59473-265-2 **$7.99** *For ages 0–4*
(A book from SkyLight Paths, Jewish Lights' sister imprint)

Also Available: **God's Paintbrush Teacher's Guide**

8½ x 11, 32 pp, PB, 978-1-879045-57-6 **$8.95**

God's Paintbrush Celebration Kit

A Spiritual Activity Kit for Teachers and Students of All Faiths, All Backgrounds
9½ x 12, 40 Full-color Activity Sheets & Teacher Folder w/ complete instructions
HC, 978-1-58023-050-6 **$21.95**
8-Student Activity Sheet Pack (40 sheets/5 sessions), 978-1-58023-058-2 **$19.95**

In God's Name

Like an ancient myth in its poetic text and vibrant illustrations, this award-winning modern fable about the search for God's name celebrates the diversity and, at the same time, the unity of all people.

9 x 12, 32 pp, Full-color illus., HC, 978-1-879045-26-2 **$16.95** *For ages 4 & up*

Also Available as a Board Book: **What Is God's Name?**

5 x 5, 24 pp, Full-color illus., Board Book, 978-1-893361-10-2 **$7.99** *For ages 0–4*
(A book from SkyLight Paths, Jewish Lights' sister imprint)

Also Available in Spanish: **El nombre de Dios**

9 x 12, 32 pp, Full-color illus., HC, 978-1-893361-63-8 **$16.95**

Noah's Wife: The Story of Naamah

When God tells Noah to bring the animals of the world onto the ark, God also calls on Naamah, Noah's wife, to save each plant on Earth. Based on an ancient text.

9 x 12, 32 pp, Full-color illus., HC, 978-1-58023-134-3 **$16.95** *For ages 4 & up*

Also Available as a Board Book: **Naamah, Noah's Wife**

5 x 5, 24 pp, Full-color illus., Board Book, 978-1-893361-56-0 **$7.95** *For ages 0–4*
(A book from SkyLight Paths, Jewish Lights' sister imprint)

For Heaven's Sake

Heaven is often found where you least expect it.

9 x 12, 32 pp, Full-color illus., HC, 978-1-58023-054-4 **$16.95** *For ages 4 & up*

God Said Amen

An inspiring story about hearing the answers to our prayers.

9 x 12, 32 pp, Full-color illus., HC, 978-1-58023-080-3 **$16.95** *For ages 4 & up*

Theology/Philosophy/The Way Into... Series

The Way Into... series offers an accessible and highly usable "guided tour" of the Jewish faith, people, history and beliefs—in total, an introduction to Judaism that will enable you to understand and interact with the sacred texts of the Jewish tradition. Each volume is written by a leading contemporary scholar and teacher, and explores one key aspect of Judaism. The Way Into... series enables all readers to achieve a real sense of Jewish cultural literacy through guided study.

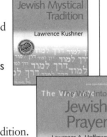

The Way Into Encountering God in Judaism
By Rabbi Neil Gillman, PhD
For everyone who wants to understand how Jews have encountered God throughout history and today.
6 x 9, 240 pp, Quality PB, 978-1-58023-199-2 **$18.99**; HC, 978-1-58023-025-4 **$21.95**
Also Available: **The Jewish Approach to God:** A Brief Introduction for Christians
By Rabbi Neil Gillman, PhD
5½ x 8½, 192 pp, Quality PB, 978-1-58023-190-9 **$16.95**

The Way Into Jewish Mystical Tradition
By Rabbi Lawrence Kushner
Allows readers to interact directly with the sacred mystical texts of the Jewish tradition. An accessible introduction to the concepts of Jewish mysticism, their religious and spiritual significance, and how they relate to life today.
6 x 9, 224 pp, Quality PB, 978-1-58023-200-5 **$18.99**; HC, 978-1-58023-029-2 **$21.95**

The Way Into Jewish Prayer
By Rabbi Lawrence A. Hoffman, PhD
Opens the door to 3,000 years of Jewish prayer, making available all anyone needs to feel at home in the Jewish way of communicating with God.
6 x 9, 208 pp, Quality PB, 978-1-58023-201-2 **$18.99**

Also Available: The Way Into Jewish Prayer Teacher's Guide
By Rabbi Jennifer Ossakow Goldsmith
8½ x 11, 42 pp, PB, 978-1-58023-345-3 **$8.99**
Download a free copy at www.jewishlights.com.

The Way Into Judaism and the Environment
By Jeremy Benstein, PhD
Explores the ways in which Judaism contributes to contemporary social-environmental issues, the extent to which Judaism is part of the problem and how it can be part of the solution.
6 x 9, 288 pp, Quality PB, 978-1-58023-368-2 **$18.99**; HC, 978-1-58023-268-5 **$24.99**

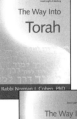

The Way Into *Tikkun Olam* (Repairing the World)
By Rabbi Elliot N. Dorff, PhD
An accessible introduction to the Jewish concept of the individual's responsibility to care for others and repair the world.
6 x 9, 304 pp, Quality PB, 978-1-58023-328-6 **$18.99**; 320 pp, HC, 978-1-58023-269-2 **$24.99**

The Way Into Torah
By Rabbi Norman J. Cohen, PhD
Helps guide in the exploration of the origins and development of Torah, explains why it should be studied and how to do it.
6 x 9, 176 pp, Quality PB, 978-1-58023-198-5 **$16.99**

The Way Into the Varieties of Jewishness
By Sylvia Barack Fishman, PhD
Explores the religious and historical understanding of what it has meant to be Jewish from ancient times to the present controversy over "Who is a Jew?"
6 x 9, 288 pp, Quality PB, 978-1-58023-367-5 **$18.99**; HC, 978-1-58023-030-8 **$24.99**

About Jewish Lights

People of all faiths and backgrounds yearn for books that attract, engage, educate, and spiritually inspire.

Our principal goal is to stimulate thought and help all people learn about who the Jewish People are, where they come from, and what the future can be made to hold. While people of our diverse Jewish heritage are the primary audience, our books speak to people in the Christian world as well and will broaden their understanding of Judaism and the roots of their own faith.

We bring to you authors who are at the forefront of spiritual thought and experience. While each has something different to say, they all say it in a voice that you can hear.

Our books are designed to welcome you and then to engage, stimulate, and inspire. We judge our success not only by whether or not our books are beautiful and commercially successful, but by whether or not they make a difference in your life.

For your information and convenience, at the back of this book we have provided a list of other Jewish Lights books you might find interesting and useful. They cover all the categories of your life:

Bar/Bat Mitzvah	Life Cycle
Bible Study / Midrash	Meditation
Children's Books	Men's Interest
Congregation Resources	Parenting
Current Events / History	Prayer / Ritual / Sacred Practice
Ecology / Environment	Social Justice
Fiction: Mystery, Science Fiction	Spirituality
Grief / Healing	Theology / Philosophy
Holidays / Holy Days	Travel
Inspiration	12-Step
Kabbalah / Mysticism / Enneagram	Women's Interest

Stuart M. Matlins, Publisher

Or phone, fax, mail or e-mail to: **JEWISH LIGHTS Publishing**
Sunset Farm Offices, Route 4 • P.O. Box 237 • Woodstock, Vermont 05091
Tel: (802) 457-4000 • Fax: (802) 457-4004 • www.jewishlights.com
Credit card orders: **(800) 962-4544** (8:30AM–5:30PM ET Monday–Friday)
Generous discounts on quantity orders. SATISFACTION GUARANTEED. Prices subject to change.